AF632850

Zephyr

H.S. Mac

BookLeaf Publishing

Presentation by *BookLeaf Publishing*

Web: www.bookleafpub.com

E-mail: info@bookleafpub.com

ISBN: 9789357213226

First edition 2023

Weeds

Weeds.
What differentiates them from a house plant?
Foliage worshiped or roughly torn from the
Earth.

Humans.
Heartbeats admired or mocked.
Based on their ability to amalgamate.

Me.
Leaves and roots
- in all the wrong places.
A weed amongst the house plants.

But I, too, feel loneliness within the solitude.
Am i not deserving of water, fertiliser and sun
on my porcelain skin?
Proudly sat in your window sill, in an ivory tin?
Merely because I grow thorns instead of lilies.

But then I ponder
on people exhaling their worries into shards of
floating dandelions.

Water the weeds.
Don't rip them from the Earth.
Regardless of how they flower -
individuality is what constitutes the Universe.

Black Ink

Two pools of obsidian black ink,
your eyes.
In a world that worships ocean blue.

Spoken in soliloquy,
your honesty.
While others are immersed in fear of truth.

Heart open wide,
your vulnerability.
Convictions perched proudly on your sleeve.

Don't morph your veracity,
into afeared ocean eyes, like me.

Coexisting Carbon Dioxide

I want to coexist in your carbon dioxide
breathing you in.
Occupy my insides with the caramel scent of
your skin.

But, how do I attract true love,
If I am not being true to myself?
Instead fitting societies mould;
material, status and wealth.

If I declare my love for the dark,
& my loathe for sandy feet,
If I rip off my mask,
What will you see?

Will you love me for the person
I am too afraid to show others?
Or will your caramel scent
Occupy the insides of another.

Friends and Furniture

This Earth is filled with evidence of our
disregard
slowly filling with items deemed not good
enough
and thus,
discard.

From what we sit on,
to what we cover ourselves with.
Our ability to throw away
even human beings,
"friends" will become a myth.

Junk Yard Beetles

Looking at a junk yard
& all I can see
is decaying commodities -
they're a reflection of me.

Underneath fetid water
& decomposing debris
A miracle is happening,
as it is, inside of me.

Two paltry beetles,
making anew.
Nearby, stands a seedling,
flora is sprouting too.

Where you are in life,
is not a reflection of where you'll always be.
Although you feel stagnant,
one day you'll be free.

You are Me.

You are safe with me,
I promise you that.
All that you've seen -
how you've been taught to act.

Together we will unravel
the cause of your pain,
We will tear your wounds open,
just to close them again.

The difference is this time,
you will be healed indelibly.
Wounded inner child,
because you are me.

Gardener's Glove

I was paltry,
until I met you.
A mere seed -
tenderly, fondly, I grew.

Through your love,
came verdant leaves and vines.
Your gentle glove –
scarlet came alive.

But something shifted
as the fruit appeared-
my leaves thickened
but your love steered.

I shiver in the shadow
of the flying creature above.
Why aren't you protecting me?
When I've given you nothing but scarlet love.

Christmas

As she declared her love for christmas,
my primal instinct was to agree.
I could falsify fondness of cinnamon trails -
throbbing lights wrapped around slain trees.

In my venture towards authenticity, I breathed "I do not...
Christmas breeds family delusion"
She looked at me, quite shocked.

The silence turned me into a Gazelle
paralyzed, realising a Lion silently awaits.
one crunch in the grass - my neck in her fangs.

The porcelain between my chin and chest
bleeding into a bright crimson
but if I had to choose each time -
- crimson blood, authenticity, disapproval, is liberation.

Inconsequential Earth

Human acceptance is the Earth;
small and insignificant.
Compared to genuine connection, the Universe,
Colossal and magnificent.

Stand firm in your authenticity.

Autopsy

As if conducting an autopsy,
dissecting you is key.
I yearn to understand your quiet corpse,
& have you know nothing of me.

My vulnerability a paradox,
being truly seen brings dread.
For, if the roles reversed,
I'd simply rather be dead.

Maybe one day,
I'll lower the guard,
and you'll explore me with a scalpel.
Until then, my dear,
love me just the same -
unaware of the truth within my skull.

Flexible Clay Cups

Not enough like you,
not enough like them.
Stuck in the middle
- no mans land.

Living here is quiet,
but living here is truth.
At peace within my solitude,
simply enjoying the view.

Of humans all around,
pretending they're flexible clay.
Moulding into unnatural shapes,
just to be the chosen cup, each day.

I invite you into no mans land,
all you cups with no handles.
And for those of you who fit the mould,
worry not, lets intertangle.

Imperfect cups and those with no flaws,
all hold black coffee the same.
So drink, sweet thing,
chip or not, individuality we reclaim.

The Power of the Tree

Amongst the emerald grass,
where the verdant trees grow.
A flightless bird, does the unknown.

In pursuit of his rival -
over something as simple as meat.
He takes a big leap,
and alas, he lands on his feet.

As he looks around,
Between clouds that promise rain,
He realises he is in the sky,
No longer with the grains.

And that, my friend,
Is a story about how,
you can reach your potential
when you challenge yourself.

Eulogy

When I take my final breath
and my bones turn to dust.
My death in words; my eulogy, will be unjust.

As strangers speak of fond memories,
they are unaware, they were merely interacting
with my inventory.

My bank of personalities,
each hand-crafted, designed with expertise.
Individuality is being extinguished
set on fire, by people like me.

I am merely a collection of all the people I have
ever known,
No idea who I am, what drives me; my
personality forever on loan.

Ivy Lineage

Your parent's rendezvous, was a fortunate act of
serendipity.
Your grandparents too, an immense
synchronicity.

These miracles climb up your lineage,
Like ivy to a wall.
So marvel in your existence
Your chance of being born, so small.

Lack of Vigilance

Words set sail from your lips, tenderly
wandering to my ears.
No longer purified through my vigilance –
my guard faded over the years.

Like an infant entrusting it's mother -
my survival depends on you.
My feeble heart in your possession,
I urge only the truth.

Grapes and Pins

Grapes, a sapid world within.
however, so fragile -
quickly sabotaged with a pin.

The honeyed extract would leak,
leaving a parched, bland mess.
Reflect on the company you keep -
the impact on you is immense.

Akin to a grape, you are delicate;
one slit could change it all.
If you surround yourself with barbed wire
your character will be mauled.

Delicate Cord

The delicate cord the sustained you,
is the same that ravages me.
As you grow older,
it heaves, seeking to set you free.

I try to catch my breath, as you need me less.
But that tug in my naval reminds me -
no song long ago, you were inside me.

It is fated to snap, one day -
when the distance between us is too far.
My arms will be empty,
our fusion only known through my scar.

So during these long days, of our bodies
intertwined.
I'll constrict the cord around both of us
Breathing you in, until it combusts.

Brood

Footless, slithering towards you
Cold hands wrapped around your skin.
Its touch chills your spine –
Last gasp, and it's in.

Death is inescapable –
Yet we attempt to elude it.
The mere thought makes us fable,
But what if we simply submit?

Let us not brood over the inevitable
when today persists.
Let your bare skin in the water,
Give that woman a burning kiss
 - you exist!

Muse

I try to find you in strangers that I see,
searching for your face on the street.

Hair made of gold,
skin radiant dew.
Green eyes, the rarest of all.
No one compares to you.

The first to have my heart
And although, since there's been others -
you left your mark,
and I am trying to recover.

My skin still burns
where your warmth touched it.
Your smell fogs my brain,
please, release me of this pain.

Timing was cruel to us -
it never quite fit.
Dancing around one another for years,
and then we were split.

Distance divided us, but you kept my heart.
Release it back to me,
or I'll keep turning you in to art.

Complex Cakes

You never truly know anyone, we all wear a
mask.
Some to progress, others for connection.
Regardless of the reason, it is simply not
genuine.

We aren't designed to fit in a box,
Antilogy is human nature;
There are layers to each of us.

You don't disregard a cake for its complexity
Stratified yet delectable
Embrace all sides of you, even those that are
messy.

You can simultaneously emit darkness and light
and change one day to the next.
Your personality doesn't have to be defined.
Remarkable human, you are complex.

Embedded in Your Youth

And with that,
an observation -
a reflection.
Of you, your authenticity,
your ability to love people regardless of their complexity.
The smile lines deeply embedded within your youth
showcase that happiness is your truth.

www.ingramcontent.com/pod-product-compliance
Lightning Source LLC
Chambersburg PA
CBHW062111140826
49812CB00058B/1303
9789357213226